RAISING THE BAR

HOW TO GIVE OUTSTANDING LEGAL PRESENTATIONS

DAVID K. FRAM, ESQ.

Printed in the United States of America
ISBN: 9781689129879
Back Cover Photo by Fabio Piccione
Edited and formatted by Trish Lewis

For information about ordering additional copies of this book, check out www.davidkfram.com

Dedicated to

John P. Fischer, Esq.

who taught me
many of the lessons
in this book,
and who mentored
a generation of lawyers
in the art
of public speaking.

WHY I WROTE THIS BOOK

We all love hearing a great presentation. It makes us feel energized and excited. And we all know that an exceptional teacher can make *any* topic fascinating.

Over the years, I have helped organize hundreds of conferences, have watched over 1,100 different speakers deliver presentations, and have read tens of thousands of evaluations of speakers.

I have personally given over 2,000 speeches at legal/association/public conferences, at in-house presentations to Fortune 500 companies, to many universities, to over 100 local and state government agencies, and to most federal agencies.

Through listening to others, reading evaluations, and speaking, I've learned many practical lessons about what works and what doesn't work in giving an effective and remarkable presentation.

I wrote this book because we all deserve to hear great presentations *and* we're all capable of being those exceptional teachers. I hope you enjoy my tips!

David K. Fram

TABLE OF CONTENTS

INTRODUCTION

Every legal professional needs to give presentations ... sometimes formal, sometimes informal. These presentations could be to many kinds of groups: colleagues, clients, potential clients, bar associations, conferences, clubs -- you name it.

Many of us give legal presentations all the time, but very few of us have ever actually been *taught* how to give an effective, compelling legal presentation (aside from litigation training).

"Yeah, yeah, yeah," says the voice in our heads. "I've been to law school. I'm smart, I'm articulate, I'm good with people. I don't need any *special* training on how to give a presentation."

Guess what? We *all* need training.

Great lawyers can often be terrible speakers. We sometimes forget the professional composition of our audience, we haven't really thought through the message we want to deliver, we run overtime (or undertime), or we confuse our audience because we haven't properly organized the talk. Sometimes, we never "capture" the audience to begin with because our opening is weak. Worst of all, we can be real bores.

Let's change that.

This book takes you through the steps and gives tips on how to prepare and deliver a powerful, unforgettable presentation. I've also included space after the tips/hints/exercises for you to take notes or write down your ideas.

Before we get started, it is essential to remember one basic point: your presentation should be a *gift* to your audience. So… give a gift. Be generous and selfless. When thinking about your audience, ask yourself, "How can I help you?" Let's care more about our audience than we care about our own egos.

As you'll see, there are many choices you'll need to make as you prepare your talk, depending on your audience and your message. Some are obvious, some less so. But always, always, *always* make intentional choices.

And have fun.

Let's go through the ten tips that I use as I prepare and deliver my own presentations. And, whenever you get stuck, re-read my earlier point … remind yourself that your presentation is your *gift*. That will get you back on track.

TIP #1
UNDERSTAND YOUR AUDIENCE

BEGIN YOUR PREPARATION BY ANALYZING YOUR AUDIENCE.

Who is your audience and what are they looking for?

- Is it your workgroup at a law firm?

- Is it a group of human resource professionals?

- Is it a group of lawyers?

- Is it a *combination* of human resource professionals and lawyers?

- Is it a rotary club or other civic organization?

Understanding who comprises your audience will affect virtually everything that follows. For example, the terminology you use if you are speaking to first-line supervisors at a private company or a county agency is completely different from what you would use if speaking to partners at a law firm. And if you are speaking to a mixed group of lawyers and others, the terminology must be understandable by everyone (without sounding too basic to those who might have more formal legal training).

In analyzing your audience, it is critical to ask yourself: "What terminology do they really use day-to-day?" It's easy when we're speaking to a group of lawyers. But if you're speaking to human resource professionals, don't assume that they will know what a term like "summary judgment" means. Explain all legal terminology (without being condescending, of course).

Hint: If you are speaking to an audience which includes non-lawyers, explain what any legal terms mean. For example, instead of saying, "The employer defeated the employee on summary judgment," you could instead say, "The employer won the case on summary judgment. What this means is that even if everything the employee said is true, the employer still didn't do anything that's illegal and the employer won the case quickly."

Really put yourselves in the shoes of an audience member. What do *they* want to hear? What do *they* want to know? What will be an exciting and effective way to speak to *them*? If you don't know these answers, do a little digging. You could make a call and ask the conference organizer these questions. It's surprising how we sometimes misunderstand what our audience really wants or needs to know and understand.

Exercise: Ask the conference organizer about particular issues that have come up for the group. What questions and issues have they actually been dealing with? Incorporate these as examples in your presentation.

If you're giving a presentation to a client, you need to know their particular "corporate speak." For example, get answers to questions like these:

- Does this client refer to itself by its full name or by its initials (Hewlett Packard or HP)?

- Does it call its worksite a "campus"?

- Does it call its supervisors "team leaders"?

- Does it call its employees "associates"?

- Does it call its departments "work groups"?

When you use the audience's terminology, you gain instant credibility. The client perceives that you understand them. Unfortunately, if you get it wrong, you can instantly lose your audience because they perceive (correctly or incorrectly) that you don't "get" them and/or you haven't made an effort to recognize their special traits.

Everything you do should be focused on keeping your audience members -- whether hourly employees, CEOs, or your boss -- interested and motivated.

Exercise: Analyze the actual composition of your audience. Ask yourself: What is each of these individuals looking to get out of my presentation? What do they want to take away? What are the special terms this audience uses that might come up in my presentation?

Understanding your audience also means respecting their culture. There are some regions and some industries that are simply more progressive or more conservative. For example, when I speak to a more culturally conservative group, I am generally careful about quoting offensive language from a court decision. Several years ago, a lawyer friend of mine learned this lesson the hard way. Several audience members approached her after her speech to say that they actually left the room for the portion of her speech where she quoted from a particularly colorful decision. She realized too late that by choosing to spice up the talk with the gratuitously crude language, she wasted an opportunity to reach those participants because they actively chose to tune her out.

Now, *having said this*, let me also point out that if the offensive language is actually necessary to understand a legal point, ignore my advice, bite the bullet, and use the crude language from the opinion.

An audience also wants respect for their industry and their geographic location. Don't ever make fun of either one. I was once giving a presentation for a plumbing supply corporation and a co-presenter made a sarcastic comment about toilets. *Ouch!* The evaluations reflected both the outrage (some reviews included jokes about *lawyers*), and the fact that some audience members stopped listening to his message after that moment.

Along these lines, it's important to remember that people generally love where they live. Although there's no *need* to praise the beauty of a particular city or region, *if* you feel it, shout it out. If you love the food, if you love the river, if you love the football team, at some relevant point during your talk, tell your audience about your affection. Even at a *legal* presentation, we are all human beings and we appreciate this kind of praise.

Understanding your audience can also require that you refrain from "bashing" people or professions with whom you disagree. For example, I have seen defense attorneys criticize a stereotyped plaintiff's attorney. Or a management attorney might criticize a stereotyped union attorney. There's no need to do this. You just need to give your best presentation and let your group reach its own conclusions about management attorneys, plaintiffs' attorneys or union attorneys. Plus, there's always a strong possibility that there *is* a management attorney, plaintiff's attorney or union attorney in that audience. Or that an audience member has a family member who is in one of those specialties.

Hint: Rather than criticize the plaintiff's attorney, it would be more effective to lay out the position that the attorney might take, and the arguments you would use to rebut that position.

Speakers sometimes have a particularly tough challenge: speaking to an audience that does *not* want to be there, but is required to attend because of an edict from above. For example, a company might require that all employees attend sexual harassment training, or an employer may have agreed to mandatory supervisory training as part of a consent decree. None of the rules outlined in this book change with regard to these audiences. But in these cases, you'll need to try even *harder* to be engaging because you have the additional challenge of winning over the audience.

Hint: Mandatory training sessions are typically well-attended (of course). The problem is that at least 90% of the group really doesn't want to be sitting there. I

sometimes start these sessions by commenting on the incredible turnout. This nearly always leads someone to shout out, "It's mandatory," which then leads to a nice chuckle among the audience. It seems to be a good ice breaker.

It also gives you a chance to then say something like, "You are going to be so happy that this training is mandatory because we're going to have so much fun together today." I sometimes go further by saying, "In fact, you're not going to want to leave at the end of the day!"

Notes from Exercises on
"Understand Your Audience"

_____

_____

_____

_____

_____

_____

_____

_____

_____

_____

_____

_____

TIP #2
WHAT IS YOUR MESSAGE?

THIS MIGHT SOUND OBVIOUS, BUT IT'S NOT.

Ask yourself these questions:

- Am I giving an update on a particular area of law to a group of lawyers?

- Am I telling my co-workers about my latest cases?

- Am I reporting on items I learned at a recent conference?

- Am I talking about strategies for a new case?

- Am I giving hints on rolling out some new corporate policy?

- Am I responding to how we are going to fix a particular problem in the workplace

- Am I trying to win over a potential client by describing my firm's depth and expertise?

- Am I teaching managers how to comply with the law?

Hint: Even if you're "just" giving a presentation to your work group, it should still be well prepared and organized, and powerfully delivered. Law firm partners have told me that when an associate is simply giving even an informal presentation, the partner is judging this person's ability to organize and communicate. So, for an associate, this is truly an opportunity to impress.

Exercise: What is your message to this audience?

Deliberately ask yourself this: When the audience walks away at the end of my speech, what do I want them thinking? Your audience should be so excited that they can't wait to tell others about what they learned. So, if your answer is, "She's very competent and professional," that's not enough of a takeaway. If your answer is, "Wow, the time just flew by and I sure learned a lot," that's much better. If your answer is, "Wow, the time just flew by, I sure learned a lot, and I can't wait to share this information," that's the best.

In delivering your message, try to appear neutral in your presentation. If you sound like you've got a strong opinion on the issue, you're likely to be less persuasive than if you present the facts and let your audience reach its own conclusions. I've seen this in evaluations of speakers at conferences I've helped organize. For example, I once watched as a healthcare benefits speaker started his talk by saying, "Obamacare is the worst law Congress ever passed." A number of participants responded on their evaluations with comments such as, "Once he said that, how could I possibly trust him to give an honest, unbiased assessment of anything else dealing with that law." In other words, how could they trust his message?

It's the same thing when a speaker is talking about judges, courts, and opinions. I've heard speakers say things such as, "This decision is just wrong," or "This judge is an idiot." In one typical evaluation a participant wrote, "Who cares whether he thinks the decision is wrong? It's still what the court said." Or speakers often say something like, "The Ninth Circuit is laughable" (or something worse). Here is what one participant wrote in response to that comment at a recent conference: "Too bad she thinks the Ninth Circuit is laughable. I still have to follow those cases. I wish she would have just told me the best arguments that I can make to the Ninth Circuit." In other words, "I wish she had given me a useful message."

Hint: If you think a court made an incorrect decision, it would be better to note the specific points where the decision conflicts with other decisions. If you think a Court of Appeals' decisions are inconsistent with other Circuits, it would be better to say that this Circuit tends to be more progressive or more conservative than other Circuits. An audience member will especially appreciate it if you can provide clever, creative arguments and approaches that might be persuasive in that Circuit.

Truly analyzing your message also will help you avoid a common mistake often made by lawyers: Telling "war stories" about their successes. Unless your message is about the story of your life and career (which it's probably not), you should avoid talking about all of your accomplishments. Yes, it's true that examples of *some* things you've worked on may be relevant. But use these examples judiciously because there are likely to be even *better* examples that come out of reported court cases. It's very transparent when you're trying to sell yourself instead of furthering your message.

Hint: Avoiding war stories also applies to talking excessively about your partners (if you're at a law firm) and their war stories.

From reading thousands of evaluations, I can tell you that participants don't want to hear about the successes of your partners. They want the message and the lessons. Again, it's transparent when a lawyer is trying to sell her firm versus giving the gift of her message.

Let the audience conclude on its own (from your incredible presentation) how great you are.

Notes from Exercise on "What is Your Message?"

_____

_____

_____

_____

_____

_____

_____

_____

_____

_____

_____

_____

TIP #3
ORGANIZE YOUR PRESENTATION FOR THIS AUDIENCE AND THIS MESSAGE

ASK YOURSELF, "WHAT IS THE MOST EFFECTIVE WAY TO PRESENT THIS MESSAGE TO THIS GROUP?"

There's no one right way to organize your presentation. The organization depends on the answers to Tip #1 and Tip #2. For example, there are many ways you can organize a legal presentation and materials. Here are some:

- Case-by-Case

- Topical

- Chronological

- Problem/Solution

Let's explore each one.

Case-by-Case

If you are simply giving an update of new cases, you might choose to list the cases and describe them.

This is often the least interesting way to organize a presentation, but it might be exactly what the audience wants, especially when you are presenting to lawyers who are attending a continuing legal education seminar and who simply need an update of the law on a particular, narrow topic.

Hint: Even though this type of presentation can be dry, you can still spice it up by giving practical take-aways from the cases you're discussing, providing interesting examples of how these lessons might apply in other cases.

Topical

This type of organization is generally much more interesting than a straight case-by-case approach. Using a topical organization, you are focused on an area of the law, and then inserting any new cases on that particular topic/subtopic.

This approach is more appropriate for a group that includes non-lawyers. Using this type of organization, you will want to get as detailed as possible on the topic/subtopic before you start listing or discussing the cases on that issue.

Hint: Remember that the legal cases you're recounting under both the case-by-case and topical organizations are all authentic stories involving actual people. So, be an exciting story-teller, describing the interesting color and detail, letting the listener truly get a mental image of the characters in the story.

Chronological

This type of organization is appropriate if you are giving a presentation about one particular case you are working on.

This gives you the chance to tell the story from beginning to end.

Hint: In using the chronological type of organization, you can build suspense because you are, in a sense, describing a drama. For example, you can give hints as to what the ending might be, teasing the audience with the possibilities.

Problem/Solution

This would be the correct way to organize your presentation if you are speaking on a particular problem in the workplace. For example, when there's been a sexual harassment issue, you could present the problem and how you are proposing to fix it.

Hint: Regardless of your choice of organization – whether case-by-case, topical, chronological, or problem/solution -- most legal presentations include handouts for the audience. It is important that your oral presentation closely follow the written materials you've handed out. Never ask the group to skip around in your written materials. Sometimes, this is a problem when a lawyer is filling in for someone else who has written the materials differently from the way the new speaker would like to present them. Think about it ahead of time. If your oral and written presentations aren't consistent, re-organize one or the other. Remember, this is a gift to your audience and you need to make it simple and easy for everyone to follow along and understand your message.

Exercise: Look at your topic and analyze the most effective way of presenting it. Ask yourself: Is there an even more creative way of presenting this topic?

Notes from Exercise on
"Organize Your Presentation"

_____

_____

_____

_____

_____

_____

_____

_____

_____

_____

_____

TIP #4
GET EXCITED ABOUT YOUR TOPIC

THERE'S SIMPLY NO SUBSTITUTE FOR PASSION.

It's inspiring when a speaker loves the topic. And it's grueling when the speaker doesn't. I've heard lawyers start speeches by saying, "I hate this law, but you need to know the new developments." *Ouch.* What participant could possibly want to hear what's coming? Remember… you're giving a gift. You wouldn't hand someone a gift and say, "I hate this gift, but I know you need it."

You *must* be excited and passionate. If you're *not*, ask yourself what you can do to become excited and passionate about the subject. Talk to someone who *is* passionate about the topic and find out why it's so much fun.

If you can't get excited or at least seem excited, let someone else give the presentation.

It's nearly impossible to tune out a speaker who is super enthusiastic about the topic.

Hint: I sometimes start a presentation by saying, "I was so excited about talking to you today that I couldn't even sleep last night!"

Forget about your ego. Forget about whether you think you seem like a "serious professional." You should be focused only on your audience members and the best way to reach them.

Too many people -- especially lawyers -- are afraid that if they don't give a presentation in a serious, academic style, they won't be respected. Frankly, these presentations are just plain boring. Have fun, use your hands, don't be afraid that someone thinks you're a little strange because you love this topic so much. In fact, make that your goal. People learn best when they're engaged and having fun.

Exercise: Are you excited about your topic? If not, what steps will you take to change this?

One lawyer friend of mine told me that when he was a junior associate, he was told by a senior partner that he should never use his hands or sound too excited when he spoke because it would make him look unprofessional. I'm here to tell you that the advice he was given was absolutely 100% wrong. Don't *ever* listen to people who tell you to contain your enthusiasm.

Studies have shown that voice excitement and body language (including eye contact) are (unfortunately!) vastly more important to an audience member than even the actual content of a speech. So, while your content should be top notch, don't miss out on these other elements that can make such a difference to your audience.

Hint: Make eye contact during your speech. This is important to both you (the speaker) and to your audience members. It is energizing to any speaker when we see an audience member nodding in agreement. In fact, if you start nodding (if it is appropriate) as you speak, you will likely find someone nodding back at you!

Keep your volume up as you speak. This will help your passion and energy shine through.

Hint: If possible, do a soundcheck before any audience member comes into the room.

Hint: If you are using a stationary podium microphone, don't wander away from it. Although this book does not cover the many decisions involved with whether a speaker should stand at a podium or walk around the room with a hand-held or lavalier microphone, there is one thing that I can say with certainty: If you step away from a stationary microphone, it will frustrate your audience because they won't be able to hear you, so be conscious of the location of the microphone at all times.

Don't read your paper to the audience. This is deadly. I completely understand that, for purposes of bolstering your confidence, you might want your presentation written out word-for-word. Even in this case, *still* don't read it to the group. Have keywords highlighted, so that you can glance down at the paper and use these as a springboard for your talk.

Hint: Always keep in mind that participants want more from you than what is in your paper. For example, give additional insights or practice pointers. Otherwise, a common refrain in participant evaluations is, "I didn't need to be here. I could have read the paper at home."

Hint: Whenever possible, I like to greet people as they're coming into the conference room. Introduce yourself and ask about the individual. It establishes an instant connection. Take some time to casually speak to people in the audience, especially in the front row and even the back rows. If you're nervous, this can help re-channel any anxiety into excitement. You can ask these folks what they're looking to learn from your presentation. And it gives you someone to look at from time to time during your talk, someone with whom you've already developed a connection.

Hint: Prepare all of your logistics ahead of time. Ask yourself what you will need (such as water or hot tea) so that once you are on stage, your focus can be solely on giving a great presentation. It's never a good idea for a speaker to stop during the presentation (for example, to ask for a glass of water) because this disrupts the flow and energy of your presentation.

Notes from Exercise on
"Get Excited About Your Topic"

_____

_____

_____

_____

_____

_____

_____

_____

_____

_____

_____

TIP #5
CONNECT INSTANTLY

YOUR FIRST WORDS SHOULD BE GRIPPING.

Connecting instantly is essential. Studies have shown that you have less than one minute to get the attention of your audience before they tune into their cell phones and tune you out.

So … start strong!

You have many choices on how to effectively begin your talk.

Here are several ideas:

Why I'm so excited to talk to you!

One option is to start your talk by enthusiastically saying that you're super excited to be with this group because *so much* has been changing in this area of the law. And if this group has some special characteristic (for example, the group is comprised of medical professionals), tell them up front why it's *especially* exciting to be talking to them because of the particular issues they handle. In this case, give short examples to get some of them to nod their heads in agreement right away.

Hint: Immediately after your opening, give the group something to write down. This is a concrete signal that you're not going to start off with fluff. It indirectly tells the group that they can't tune out and that they need to start actively listening right away.

Engage with A Dramatic Statistic

Consider immediately opening your talk with some surprising statistic (jury verdicts, number of new reported cases on this issue, number of charges filed with an enforcement agency). For example, instead of starting off by saying, "We're going to be talking about developments in sexual harassment law," start with, "Last year, U.S. companies paid over $1 billion in sexual harassment settlements. And can you even imagine how much those companies paid in legal fees? Anyone want to take a guess?"

Engage Immediately with a Question

Another option is to start your talk by asking people to raise their hands if they've had a particular issue come up. If you do this, be sure to use an example that will elicit a response.

Hint: People are more likely to participate in this type of exercise if you include yourself in the survey. For example, rather than saying, "How many of you have been asked by an employee whether they can bring a comfort animal to work?" say this, "How many of us have been asked by an employee..." (while you yourself raise your hand).

Or, ask the group a relevant question. For example, "Does anyone want to take a guess at how many states prohibited discrimination based on sexual orientation 30 years ago? Now, take a guess at how many states prohibit sexual orientation discrimination today?"

Hint: If no one responds, you can revert back to the prior example and ask, "How many of us think that the answer is none?" Then, pause. Then, "How many think the answer is less than five?" And so on.

Engage Immediately with a Visual

You might choose to start your speech with some dramatic visual. For example, an associate I once coached told me that he didn't know how to start his planned presentation on biometrics in the workplace. Together, we came up with the idea of starting his presentation by projecting a highly magnified photograph of a human eye. He then asked the audience what they thought it was. Some guessed that it was a mountain range. Some guessed it was a flower. Then, he slowly advanced the slides as the image zoomed out more and more until it was finally recognizable as an eye. Then, he explained how eye scans are being used more and more to identify employees in the workplace.

How *NOT* to Start a Presentation

Never, *ever, **ever*** (did I make the point?) start a speech by explaining why the presentation is *not* going to be great. Here are some examples of opening lines I have heard lawyers use over the years:

> "As I was driving over here, I was thinking about what to say."

> "I'm not exactly sure how I'm going to fill two full hours on this topic."

> "I know I'm substituting for [name of speaker] who can't be here, and I know I can't really fill her shoes."

> "Not much has changed in this area of the law."

Did you hear yourself in any of those openings? Or do you remember a speaker starting a talk like this? They've effectively just told you that they're not prepared, that you don't need to listen to the presentation, and/or they've pleaded with you,

"*Please* don't expect too much of me because I'm not going to be very good."

Hint: Even if not much has changed in a particular area of the law, can't you reframe this in a positive light? For example, "When we look at the issues of x, y, and z, it's important to know not only what has changed, but also what hasn't changed. We're going to talk about both!"

Exercise: Brainstorm two or three ideas on how you could start your presentation (using the techniques identified above).

Notes from Exercise on
"Connect Instantly"

TIP #6
EXPLAIN YOUR ROADMAP

TELL YOUR AUDIENCE WHERE YOU'LL BE TAKING THEM.

Every professional speaker knows the traditional formula for giving your audience the roadmap for the presentation. I think of the formula as this:

Tell them.

Tell them.

Tell them.

First, tell the audience what you're going to present.

Then, actually tell them the information during the course of the presentation.

And, at the end of the talk, tell them what they've just heard.

Don't assume that your audience can read your mind or that they organize things the way you do.

This gives your audience the big picture and how all of the details fit into that picture. Plus, it lets participants feel like they've gotten a complete, tidy package to take away.

Remember, you're doing everything you can to make this an easy, fun journey.

Hint: As you prepare to tell them, tell them, tell them, this forces you to make deliberate choices in the organization of your presentation.

Hint: Repetition helps participants retain information.

Exercise: Even before you construct the central content of your presentation on your topic, write out the actual words you will use to tell them, tell them, tell them.

Notes from Exercise on "Explain Your Roadmap"

_____

_____

_____

_____

_____

_____

_____

_____

_____

_____

_____

TIP #7
BREAK
IT UP

UNDERSTAND THAT NOBODY PAYS ATTENTION FOR VERY LONG.

Most of us aren't surprised to learn that adults have a relatively short attention span. Studies show that most of us last for about 15 or 20 minutes before we start looking for some distraction. "Look, there's a squirrel!" or, more commonly in today's world, "I'd better check my emails!"

This is challenging for any speaker because most legal presentations last longer than 15-20 minutes. What should we do to keep the audience from tuning us out?

It's simple. Break it up.

There are many ways you can do this.

Every 15 or 20 minutes, you could give a "pop quiz," asking participants to raise their hands. If you like being playful, you could even give people a prize for the right answer. Or, when you get to a particularly hot topic, you could ask the audience, by a show of hands, how many participants have ever had to deal with that question. Or you could show a relevant video. Or you could do a case study.

Another option is to break up the speech by telling a true story about yourself that relates to the topic and lets the audience know *you* a little bit better. For example, I have watched a great wage and hour speaker talk about her job as a teenager frying chicken in a fast-food restaurant. She described the colorful details of what she was wearing, what she was smelling, the heat of the kitchen, what the customers were ordering, etc. She then powerfully (and often comically) discussed how the law's provisions would have applied to the various aspects of her job.

Personally, I like to sometimes break up my presentations with funny, somewhat relevant stories about my nephew, Max. For example, I point out that Max is the same age as the Americans with Disabilities Act, the topic of most of my presentations. I then talk about the times I would babysit for Max as a toddler and how I would read to him the latest Court of Appeals cases instead of reading a bedtime story (and how much he loved it!). This gives participants a chance to smile and to rest from what can sometimes be fast-paced, legally dense presentations.

Hint: Letting the audience in on a piece of your life humanizes you and lets participants relate to you. Many participants who come back to my conferences on an annual basis often ask me about Max!

By doing any of these things, you are getting your audience out of the mode of just passively sitting and listening.

Exercise: How could you break up your topic? Come up with two or three different ideas.

Notes from Exercise on
"Break it Up"

_____

_____

_____

_____

_____

_____

_____

_____

_____

_____

TIP #8
ONLY USE VISUALS THAT ENHANCE YOUR PRESENTATION

USE VISUALS SPARINGLY AND WISELY.

Visuals, like PowerPoint or Keynote, should only, *only*, **only** be used when they actually enhance your presentation. They should be used solely when they are helpful to your audience.

How many times have you heard a speaker say this: "I know you might not be able to see this slide from the back of the room."

Even though I try to use my best poker face when I hear a speaker say this, my reaction as an audience member probably looks more like Edvard Munch's *The Scream*.

Why would a speaker use a visual that can't be seen by some audience members? Why in the world would anyone use a visual aide that you *know* (in advance!) detracts from your presentation?

I'll tell you why legal speakers do it anyway. They think an audience can't possibly pay attention without seeing words flashing on a screen. Or the speaker wants a memory crutch (instead of using notes). Or it's part of the speaker's firm's branding.

These are all bad reasons to use slides.

Some of the best speakers in the history of the world haven't used PowerPoint. Could you imagine Obama or Reagan using PowerPoint? Would it have helped Martin Luther King's message if the words "I HAVE A DREAM" had popped onto a screen behind him (in some type of sunburst style) as he was standing at the Lincoln Memorial?

So ... before you incorporate slides or video into your presentation, ask yourself this: Why am I using a visual? Will this actually enhance my presentation? Will it make it easier for an audience member to understand and use my information?

Remember, this is *supposed* to be a gift to your audience.

Why Use Visuals?

No matter what you've been told, an audience does not need to stare at colorful words or images on a screen. You can be riveting without that.

The point of a visual should be to communicate something that you can't effectively communicate orally. Or to emphasize something you've said.

For example, a slide might contain short bullet points that sum up what you've said or are about to say. Or, the slide might show the audience the overall structure and organization of your talk, and where you currently are *within* that bigger framework.

Here's What Not to Do

Don't have a slide that just duplicates what you're saying orally. We've all sat through presentations like this, and it's tough for a participant to listen to you and try to read the screen (and take notes too!).

It's much better if the slide simply has some key words that you want to emphasize.

Don't have a slide that requires the audience to read words that are slightly different from what you're saying orally. Our brains just don't work that way. No matter what we think we're capable of doing, no one can effectively listen to your spoken words while reading something that's different.

In fact, if a speaker uses a slide with detailed text and bullets, the listener immediately tunes out of what's being said to try to read and process what's being projected.

Keep it Simple

Keep each slide very simple, with just one message. Ideally, as I mentioned earlier, you should have only a few keywords on the slide that emphasize what you're saying orally. If you have too much information on the slide, your audience will read instead of listening. In that case, your slide is not enhancing your presentation.

Don't jumble up the slide with different fonts and colors. Stick with one font, and only use one or two colors. Otherwise, your slide will look unprofessional and badly designed. Worse yet, it will actually detract from what you're saying.

Hint: Speakers like using the special effects of PowerPoint and Keynote for a "wow" effect. This is a bad idea. No one is impressed anymore by text that bursts onto the screen in a lightning bolt or circles onto the screen in a cyclone. Even though we might have had fun creating that slide, the result looks unsophisticated.

Size Matters

Our eyes are naturally drawn to the largest object on the screen.

Be sure that the largest text or image is the item on which you want the audience to focus. If the heading isn't the most important thing, then don't have the heading in the largest font.

And as I mentioned earlier, **never** use small writing that an audience member can't see from the back of the room.

Background Color

Ask yourself, "What is the most pleasing background color for a slide?" Is it white, or is it something darker? Many legal speakers use white, primarily because they haven't considered the alternatives.

Guess what? It's way more stressful on our eyes to be staring at a white screen. So, make it easier on your audience.

Also, a bright, white screen will immediately divert eyes from you. Remember, your slides are supposed to enhance what you're saying. They're not supposed to take attention away from you.

Hint: I always use a muted green/grey background with white lettering. I find it to be easy on the eyes.

Exercise: Experiment by preparing slides with different background colors. Show these slides to some of your colleagues and friends to get their input.

How Many Thoughts Should I Put on Each Slide?

Many of us overload our slides with too much information. Have you seen slides with too much text?

I've heard experts in the field recommend that you include no more than six items or bullet points on a screen at any one time. I would actually recommend no more than five to keep it even simpler. And, as you get to each of the five items, I would have a new slide which has that particular item in **bold**. It makes it easier for someone to pay attention to you and it lets the visual enhance what you're saying.

When I gave this advice to a senior associate I once coached, his response was, "Are you kidding me? You want me to have to have five separate slides instead of just one? That's too much work." Here's what I think: If you are using your slides to help your audience, then put in that extra effort up front.

Exercise: What words or bullet points do you want to put on a slide? How can you condense those items? What would you put in bold? How many slides will you actually need to let these slides best enhance your spoken word?

Notes from Exercise on
"Only Use Visuals That Enhance"

_____

_____

_____

_____

_____

_____

_____

_____

_____

_____

_____

TIP #9
WATCH YOUR TIMING

PACE YOURSELF AND STAY WITHIN YOUR TIMEFRAME.

It's super important to know exactly how much time you have been allocated. And it is essential to know whether this amount of time has changed for reasons beyond your control (for example, a prior speaker has unfortunately run over her allotted time).

Stating the obvious: Always stay within *your* allocated time slot. Never run over, not even if your timeframe has just been shortened.

Hint: Know your materials well enough that you are aware of exactly what could be cut or condensed if needed.

Hint: Know exactly where you should be, time-wise, in your presentation, down to 5-10 minute increments. If you see that you are falling behind, get back on track during the central part of your presentation. Don't wait until the end to fix this. It's a common error for speakers to realize towards the end of the talk that they have 30 minutes of materials to talk about and only 10 minutes remaining.

Keeping track as you go along helps you avoid that. So, have notes in the margins of your materials telling you where you want to be at what time.

Unfortunately, what I've talked about above isn't always what happens in the real world. Sometimes, our pacing isn't exactly as we planned it and we do run out of time. If that happens, you *never* want to tell the audience that you're running out of time. Or that you're going to skip pages. Otherwise, every audience member will feel cheated out of material.

They have no way of knowing whether the material you've skipped (or not gotten to) is even particularly important. All they know is that you're not giving them the gift you had promised or planned to give. Who would feel good about that?

Hint: If your time has gotten away from you, there is something you can do. Instead of saying, "We're going to skip pages 50-75," say "Pages 50-75 have some additional supplementary material for you to take a look at on your own. Now, let's turn to page 76." That way, nobody feels cheated. In fact, participants will feel like you are giving them an additional gift of supplementary materials.

I think it is more dynamic to take questions as the presentation goes along, rather than at the end.

Hint: If you take questions from the audience, it is essential that you repeat the questions back to the audience. In a large group setting, I have almost never heard an audience member ask a question loudly enough to be understood by everyone in the room. It's so much nicer for a speaker to proactively repeat the question into the microphone instead of waiting for the inevitable cry from the back of the room, "We couldn't hear the question!"

If you do take questions during your presentation, be sure to manage them effectively or they can throw off your timing.

Hint: If you see that the questions will affect your timing, you can say, "I see that a number of you still have questions. I'll need to hold off on those questions so that we can get through everything. But I'll be around afterwards to talk to any of you."

Hint: I've often been at the very end of my presentation and a questioner's hand (often in the front row) shoots up. The dilemma is that you want to call on that person (and everyone in the room has seen the hand shoot up), but you are simply out of time. So, here's the answer: Don't call on the person because it will throw off your timing and the timing of the next speaker. In these situations, I say, "I see that some of you have more questions, but we're unfortunately at the end of my time slot. Be sure to stick around and we can chat later." Then, continue with your closing, as discussed in Tip #10.

Taking questions during your talk also requires that you control the content of the discussion. For example, unless you watch it, questions can force you to stray from the carefully-planned organization of your presentation.

Hint: If someone asks a question on a topic that you're going to get to later in the presentation, don't move to that topic prematurely. Rather, say, "That's a great question and we're going to get to that issue in just a few minutes."

Sometimes, a participant decides to take control of the room and asks follow-up after follow-up (after follow-up).

In these cases, you need to politely reassert control, telling the questioner that this sounds like something you should talk about with him one-on-one after the presentation.

Exercise: What strategies will you use to effectively watch your timing?

Notes from Exercise on "Watch Your Timing""

_____

_____

_____

_____

_____

_____

_____

_____

_____

_____

_____

TIP #10
END
STRONG

PREPARE AND WRITE OUT YOUR CLOSING LINE AHEAD OF TIME.

How will you end your talk?

Many speakers have a great presentation, but then, they have no prepared conclusion. At the end of the presentation, they just say something like, "I see my time is up. So, thanks." Or, "Well …ok. That's it."

Don't do that.

"Let me thank the sponsors …."

Don't do that either (at least, not at the very end).

End with a bang!

First, include the final "tell them" (Tip #6) in your closing. In other words, tell the audience what you've just told them by summarizing your key points. In your closing, it also can be inspiring if you give your audience a call to action. This involves letting them know what they should now do with the information (the gift) that you've just given them.

Your final line should make it crystal clear that this is now the right time to applaud. At a *minimum*, you can say something like, "You're a wonderful group and it's been such a pleasure to discuss this topic with you!"

I highly recommend that you have your closing line written down and placed next to your speaking notes so that when you need it, you can quickly refer to it (instead of trying to remember your carefully constructed words in the heat of those last moments on stage).

Hint: Your final line should never be, "Are there any questions?" Unfortunately, many legal speakers do this. Even if there actually are any questions, it ends your powerful presentation with a whimper.

So, if you've held off on questions until the end, you should still have your prepared written closing line ready to go at the end of the question and answer period.

Exercise: Prepare several ways that you can close your presentation with a bang. Try these out on colleagues.

Notes from Exercise on "End Strong"

_____

_____

_____

_____

_____

_____

_____

_____

_____

_____

_____

_____

AND FINALLY...

None of this is rocket science. But it does require that you act deliberately in your preparation and presentation.

Hint: I think it's a great idea to film yourself giving a rehearsal of the talk. I know ... it's awful to watch yourself speaking. However, this is your chance to recognize that you say or do things that you'd rather not say or do, such as saying, "you know," "ummmm," "like," "actually," or "the truth is" (over and over), smacking your lips together, saying each line as if it's a question, etc. We can all learn something by watching ourselves in action, even though it's painful.

And, along these lines ... practice, practice, practice.

Never "wing" it. Give your presentation to a friend or colleague and get honest feedback. Don't be too proud. Incorporate these thoughts if you think it makes your presentation stronger. Something that was obvious to you might be lost on someone else.

This gives you the chance to refine your content and improve your presentation skills.

Keep in mind that it's a gift to *you* that *you* were chosen to speak. And what you're giving is a gift in return.

General Notes

_____

_____

_____

_____

_____

_____

_____

_____

_____

_____

_____

_____

RESOURCES

There are many great books, videos, and studies that deal with public speaking and that I have relied upon over the years. Here are some of my favorites:

Chris Anderson, TED Talks: The Official TED Guide to Public Speaking (2017)

Steve Bustin, The Authority Guide to Presenting and Public Speaking: How to Deliver Engaging and Effective Business Presentations (2016)

Ron Hoff, I Can See You Naked: A Fearless Guide to Making Great Presentations (2014)

Albert Mehrabian's writings on the "7-38-55 Rule of Personal Communication" (Publications starting in 1971)

David JP Philips, "How to Avoid Death by PowerPoint" (TEDx Talk, Stockholm 2014)

THANK YOU

There are many people to thank for guiding and supporting me over the decades that I have been giving legal presentations. I am grateful to David Robb Cralle and my parents, Sandy and Manny Fram for their unconditional love and support, my sister Debby for the lifetime of her wise advice, my brother Jeffrey for being my first role model in public speaking, supervisors like Patricia Ambrose and Peggy Mastroianni for teaching me about practical legal writing and speaking, the entire team at National Employment Law Institute for being the bedrock for everything I get to do, friends who provided feedback on this book, and the National Speakers Association for providing inspiration and training. The list could go on and on.

ABOUT THE AUTHOR

David Fram *would* be an internationally-known pop artist and Academy Award nominated actor if he had musical or acting talent. Instead, he is an attorney who loves public speaking and teaching about employment law for the National Employment Law Institute. David also is passionate about coaching attorneys to be better speakers.

He has given more than 2,000 speeches to groups around the United States, from local governments to federal agencies to many Fortune 500 companies. He has published articles in a wide variety of trade publications as well as The New York Times and The Wall Street Journal, and has written a legal treatise (now in its 47th edition) on the Americans with Disabilities Act.

ADDITIONAL INFORMATION

Please check out **davidkfram.com** for additional information about:

- Ordering copies of this book (including at a bulk discount)

- Consulting with David as a speaking coach or to arrange a class

- Consulting with David to speak to your organization on his legal area of expertise, the Americans with Disabilities Act